Come close to Christ!

Psychologist and Spiritual Director Bill Gaultiere guides you on a prayer walk with Jesus and the stations of his cross.

You'll be encouraged by

- Fresh re-tellings of Gospel stories
- Surprising insights from the Bible
- Personal reflection questions
- A hope-filled journey with Jesus

This guide is for your personal devotions or to share with friends in a small group or on a retreat. It's great for Lent or anytime of year. Appendix One features an outline for eight messages or studies.

Readers of *Unforsaken* say:

"I was overwhelmed with the love of Christ!"

"Doing the stations was the most meaningful part of the retreat for me."

"Jesus' suffering tempts me to think that God seems mean and to shut down emotionally. But *Unforsaken* shows me that actually God is caring for Jesus and for me."

"I see how I can be more like Jesus."

"Tears flowed! Seeing Jesus' sacrifice I received a deep healing for the abuse I went through."

"I can't wait to share this with my friends!"

Bill Gaultiere, PhD is the author of *Your Best Life in Jesus' Easy Yoke: Rhythms of Grace to De-Stress and Live Empowered.* He and his wife Kristi lead the ministry of Soul Shepherding to cultivate intimacy with Jesus for pastors and leaders. They and their Associates offer counseling, spiritual direction, retreats, and a certificate training program. They have three adult children and live in Irvine, CA.

Unforsaken!

With Jesus

On the Stations of the Cross

By Bill Gaultiere

Scripture meditations for devotions,
retreats, or small groups. Great for Lent!

Soul Shepherding Inc.
4000 Barranca Parkway, Suite 250
Irvine, CA 92604

© 2016 by Bill Gaultiere (text and photography).

All Scripture quotations, unless otherwise indicated, are taken from the Holy Bible, New International Version®, NIV®. Copyright ©1973, 1978, 1984, 2011 by Biblica, Inc.™ Used by permission of Zondervan. All rights reserved worldwide. www.zondervan.com The "NIV" and "New International Version" are trademarks registered in the United States Patent and Trademark Office by Biblica, Inc.™

Visit SoulShepherding.org for hundreds of free resources like devotionals, experiences for groups and retreats, and messages on audio and video.

Podcast: "Soul Talks With Bill & Kristi Gaultiere"

Devotionals: SoulShepherding.org/email-subscriptions

Social Media: On Facebook you can follow Soul Shepherding or Bill Gaultiere. On Twitter you can follow Bill Gaultiere. On Pinterest or Instagram you can follow Soul Shepherding.

Certificate Training: Soul Shepherding offers a two-year TLC certificate training program in "Christian Spiritual Formation and Soul Care Ministry" for pastors and leaders. This features four retreats of five days in a beautiful and relaxing venue in Southern California.

Discounts on Large Orders: Contact us through our website for savings on orders of ten or more books. All royalties for this book go to support the care of pastors through Soul Shepherding, Inc., a 501c3 nonprofit corporation in the State of California.

Dedication

To Kristi, my precious wife and soul mate.

Thank you for sharing yourself so authentically with me.

Your sensitivity and compassion for the pain of others is a burden you bear so beautifully. It's challenged me to keep trusting the tender mercy of God for all people — especially to Jesus in his Passion and us who meet him there.

Together with Jesus at the cross we are forever *Unforsaken!*

Contents

A Prayer For You   1

Preface: An Ancient Devotional Practice   2

Introduction: A Walk With Jesus   8

1. Jesus On Trial   14
2. Jesus Takes Up His Cross   17
3. Jesus Falls   20
4. Mary Comes to Jesus   23
5. Simon "Helps" Jesus Carry His Cross   26
6. Veronica Wipes Jesus' Face   29
7. Jesus Falls Again   32
8. Jesus Comforts the Weeping Women   35
9. Jesus Falls a Third Time   39
10. The Soldiers Strip and Abuse Jesus   42

11. Jesus is Crucified With Two Thieves   46

12. Mary and John Watch Jesus Die   49

13. Jesus Dies   53

14. Joseph Puts Jesus' Body In His Tomb   57

15. Jesus Rises From the Dead!   60

Appendix 1: Using *Unforsaken* in Lent   64

Appendix 2: Scriptural Way of the Cross   66

A Prayer For You

Unforsaken is my prayer for you.

I wrote it to introduce this ancient cross walk to more people. It features over 70 citations from the Bible that tell the life-changing story of our Lord and Savior Jesus Christ going to the cross to forgive our sins and reconcile us to God.

This booklet is field tested. It's been re-written a number of times based on what I've learned from twelve years of personal devotions and sharing it with people for retreats, Ash Wednesday and Holy Week services, Lent, and private meditation.

Let's pray...

Dear Father God, cause the Passion of Christ to become a living Gospel story for us to participate in. Open your heavenly kingdom to us. May we know with confidence that with Jesus at the Cross we are *Unforsaken!*

Preface

An Ancient Devotional Practice

I'll never forget walking the Via Dolorosa in Jerusalem. It's a street in Israel with a Latin name that means "Way of Suffering." This ancient stone-paved Roman Road has the original Stations of the Cross that commemorate Jesus carrying his cross from Pilate's house to Calvary's hill.

Over the centuries many millions of pilgrims from all around the world have done this devotional prayer walk on the Via Dolorosa. Thousands more would do it the day I was there, but I wanted to be alone as I met my Lord at his cross so I awoke well before dawn.

It was pitch black and eerie as I entered the walls of the Old City looking for the first Station. Stray cats were whining and darting back and forth in the shadows. I turned a corner and heard a commotion of crows picking at garbage strewn about. Howling dogs announced that their turn was next.

Suddenly, a drunk man staggered out of an alley and startled me! Then dozens of Jews dressed in black coats and hats flooded out of a building right in front of me. When the way was clear I walked on and came to an intersection with Israeli soldiers carrying machine guns and standing guard — I went the other way!

I continued on but I couldn't find The Stations. Suddenly, a man started yelling in Arabic over loud speakers. I covered my ears. Just then a horde of Muslims marched towards me to answer their call to prayer. I stepped aside and pressed my body into the wall of a store to keep from being trampled!

Where is the One I love? I prayed. *Where is Jesus my Lord? Where are his Stations?*

Soon I heard church bells ringing. I followed the sound which led me to turn down a different street. There I saw a priest carrying a large cross followed by people chanting prayers in Latin. *They're doing The Stations of the Cross! Thank you Lord!*

It's always been this way: *we find the Cross walk of Jesus when someone introduces us to it.* We need Christian community. We need a guide.

Ever since the resurrection of Jesus Christ people have been spreading to others the Good News that he died for our sins and rose again! The Stations of the Cross help us to do this.

In the 4th Century Jerome wrote about pilgrims from around the world traveling to

Jerusalem to visit the holy sites connected with Jesus, especially the places where he took up his cross, carried it through the city streets, and was crucified. They made carvings and drew pictures to record these events and brought them home to share with others. Their visual images helped them to tell the story, meditate on the associated Bible passages, and to pray.

Early in the 13th Century St. Francis of Assisi promoted pilgrimages to the "Via Sacra" (sacred route) in Jerusalem and emphasized this devotional practice of meditating on the Passion of Christ. Later his followers started building outdoor replicas of The Stations throughout Europe.

The traditional form of the fourteen Stations of the Cross was in place by the 17th Century. On Jerusalem's Via Dolorosa street it's a walk of not quite half a mile from the Antonia Fortress to Golgotha (which is now inside the Church of the Holy Sepulchre). In 1731 Pope Clement XII approved for The Stations to be reproduced in local churches.

Today The Stations can be found in Roman Catholic churches and monasteries around the world, as well as in a number of Anglican, Lutheran, and Methodist churches. Plaques or statues are placed in a succession of shelters along an outdoor prayer walk or a wall inside the church sanctuary.

As I describe in Appendix 2, in recent years some Christians have used adaptations of the Stations of the Cross that use only historical accounts from the Bible.

I prefer using the traditional stations in this booklet, even though some legends are included. I've found that this account of Christ's Passion fosters a deep personal engagement and transformation. Furthermore, wherever you live you can find these stations and take the same prayer walk that millions of Christians have done throughout history.

Sadly, most Christians today have never prayed The Stations. Others have looked at them or read a guide, but without much understanding.

Unforsaken emphasizes Bible teachings associated with Jesus taking up his cross and inviting us to follow him in the way of love.

It takes you back 2,000 years ago and puts you at the cross of Christ with Peter, Mary his mother, Simon of Cyrene, John his beloved disciple, and Joseph of Arimathea.

Close to Christ Jesus you'll appreciate anew that God forgives your sins and will never forsake you.

Introduction

A Walk With Jesus

Come with me on "The Way of the Cross."

It's spring of 2005 and I'm with some friends of mine on retreat at a Benedictine monastery called the Prince of Peace Abbey in Oceanside, CA.

Frannie says to us, "Let's do the Stations of the Cross."

"I thought they were only for Catholics?" Doug remarks, saying what we're all thinking. (We're part of Reformed church.)

"That's where I learned them," Frannie smiles. "But they're meant for everyone!"

"Let's try it!" I exclaim.

We decide to keep silence and go at our own pace...

Standing at the entrance to the monastery's 3/4 mile prayer walk, I recall Jesus' words: "Whoever wants to be my disciple must deny themselves and take up their cross daily and follow me" (Luke 9:23).

Thank you Jesus, I pray. *By your cross you gave us your life and showed us how to live.* (I was praying to grow in my appreciation for Christ's sacrifice *and* my apprenticeship to him in daily life.)

Then I walk to the first station and pause to pray quietly in front of the statue of Jesus being condemned by Pilate. I look into his eyes...

Jesus loves the Roman procurator. He isn't angry. Nor is he defensive. He's standing tall, confident, and secure.

How? Where does Jesus get this peace and power?

Suddenly I realize, Jesus isn't just in Pilate's palace — he's in his Father's world!

But when I'm judged I feel inadequate and insecure...

Lord Jesus, I don't know how to stand with you in God's kingdom of righteousness, peace, and joy. (Romans 14:17)

I feel teary. Holy desire wells up in my heart...

O Jesus, I want to stay close to you and become more like you!

Station after station, each depicted in a porcelain plaque, draws me to follow in Jesus' steps.

As he takes up his cross and carries it through the streets of the Old City I feel the weight and stagger with him. I wince at hearing the insults. I flinch at the crack of the whip. It's too much for me and I start to shut down emotionally.

But then I find comfort in the endearing exchange between Jesus and his mother Mary.

Still walking right behind Jesus, I cry out when he falls to the ground under the weight of the cross. I think about how often I fall down. I fall in pain. I fall in sin. I fall in failure and discouragement. Jesus never sinned, but he feels my temptations, my limitations, my struggles.

Three times Jesus falls! I want to help him, but I feel so helpless.

But Simon of Cyrene comes to help Jesus carry his cross and Veronica gives him a cloth to wipe the sweat and blood off his face.

I realize that it encourages Jesus when I take up my cross and follow him. It blesses my Lord when I offer a simple act of kindness to someone for his sake.

Then Jesus is stripped. He endures more insults and abuse. He's nailed to the cross. He cries out in pain. He's suffocating.

It's dark.

He seems alone and abandoned. The few of his followers who are watching from a distance are in despair. I feel despair too.

But then Jesus connects his beloved mother and disciple to be as mother and son. I recall that *Jesus is one with the Father.* Strengthened in this loving intimacy, he cares for everyone around him — including me — and invites us into their oneness! (John 10:30, 17:21)

He's forgiving me of my sins and reconciling me to God. He wants this for everyone — and so do I!

He's showing us that by relying on his grace we too can learn to have joy, peace, and power in our trials and to love our enemies.

Next I see Joseph of Amimathea place Jesus' body in the tomb. I enter the tomb. I reflect on my death that could come anytime.

Finally, I walk to the last Station which is on a bluff overlooking the valley below. I stand before an enormous white cross on a hill with an expansive blue sky behind it. I celebrate that "Christ is risen!"

Our Lord and Savior has overcome sin, death, and hell! He has brought us new life for all eternity!

Eager to learn more about the Stations of the Cross, I go straight into the Catholic bookstore at the monastery and buy some booklets. Right away I look up the Bible passages that relate to each station.

Then I wrote my own guide to use and shared it with others.

Now it's in your hands.

With Jesus you are *Unforsaken!*

14 *Unforsaken!*

1st Station
Jesus On Trial

*Thank you Jesus! By your cross
you gave us your life and showed us
how to live free of condemnation.*

Meditation

"The chief priests accused [Jesus] of many things. So again Pilate asked him, 'Aren't you going to answer? See how many things they are accusing you of.' But Jesus still made no reply, and Pilate was amazed." (Mark 15:3-5)

"There is now no condemnation for those who are in Christ Jesus" (Romans 8:1).

~

Jesus is judged by the high priest, then the whole Sanhedrin, then Pilate, then Herod, and then back to Pilate again. The religious leaders tell lies to Pilate and stir up the crowds to keep shouting with contempt, "Crucify him!... Crucify him!" (Mark 15:13-14)

His disciples have abandoned him. He stands alone, condemned as a criminal.

But Jesus doesn't retort. He doesn't become fearful or sullen. He doesn't slouch in shame. He isn't even defensive.

Jesus stands in silence before his accusers.

Forsaken by everyone, he remains quiet, calm, and confident. His mission is to sacrifice his life in love for all who will receive him.

How can Jesus be secure when all his friends have abandoned him to his enemies?

How does he remain at peace when he's being criticized and mistreated?

How does he keep loving his enemies who are abusing him and threatening to kill him?

The Bible says that Christ was tempted and tried as we are (Matthew 4:1-11; Hebrews 4:15). He could've sinned. He could've fallen apart emotionally. He could've internalized shame or reacted with unkind anger.

How did he suffer with such strength and grace?

In his Father's embrace, Jesus is *Unforsaken*.

This is for you. It's for everyone.

Prayer

Recall a time that you felt judged by someone and share your feelings with God...

Then recall a time that you judged someone else and pray about this...

Now stand with Jesus in the Father's world of righteousness and peace and give thanks that you're free from condemnation...

2nd Station
Jesus Takes Up His Cross

*Thank you Jesus! By your cross
you gave us your life and showed us
how to deny our self and live in God.*

Meditation

"Carrying his own cross, [Jesus] went out to the place of the Skull..." (John 19:17)

"For the joy set before him [Jesus] endured the cross..." (Hebrews 12:2)

~

Jesus is bruised and bleeding from being brutally scourged, almost to the point of death. He staggers under the weight of the cross as he stumbles through the city streets of Jerusalem.

Yet, he has a source of *joy!*

How could this be when he's in so much pain? When he's knowingly walking to the Place of the Skull where he'll be tortured to death?

Joy is more than a feeling; like love, it's a *condition of being* that goes beyond our emotions to also include our attitude, will, bodily habits, and relational connections (Mark 12:30-31). While Jesus is suffering he is drawing on his Father's love and all the wonderful treasures of the unseen Kingdom of the Heavens (Matthew 13:44-45, 52).

Truly, "The Kingdom of God is... righteousness, peace, and joy in the Holy Spirit." (Romans 14:17)

Jesus invites you to take up your cross and follow him. This cross is not bad things that happen to you — it's choosing an *attitude* of self-denial and dependence upon God in your daily life, including when bad things happen to you.

Renouncing the world opens up the heavens to us! Losing life on our own terms enables us to gain life on God's terms: *a thriving, divine life forever!* (Luke 9:23-27)

Prayer

Reflect on an example of how you could take up your cross with Jesus by denying yourself something that competes with your love for God...

Pray to enjoy being forgiven and enlivened by Christ so that you'll have the strength to take up your cross and give your all to loving God and others...

20 *Unforsaken!*

3rd Station
Jesus Falls

*Thank you Jesus! By your cross
you gave us your life and showed us
how to fall into Abba's arms of love.*

Meditation

"I am bowed down and brought very low... my strength fails me..." (Psalm 38:6, 10).

~

Apparently, as Jesus is carrying his cross he falls under the weight of it and needs help to carry it to Golgotha (Mark 15:21-22). The one who is fully God is also fully man.

This scene recalls the Garden of Gethsemane. Just before taking up his cross, Jesus feels "deeply distressed and troubled... overwhelmed with sorrow to the point of death" (Mark 14:33-34).

He falls to the ground and wrestles in prayer so intensely that he sweats drops of blood (Luke 22:44). He pleads that "the hour might pass from him." He cries out, *"Abba, Father... Take this cup from me."* (Mark 14:35-36)

We might think Jesus is trying to get out of going to the cross, but actually, as he said repeatedly, *he is trying to make it to the cross!* (Mark 8:34; 9:31; 10:33-34; 10:45; 12:1-12; 14:8; 14:22-25. See also John 12:27-28.)

It seems that Satan was trying to kill Jesus in the secrecy of the garden. But the Bible says that Jesus' prayer with loud cries and tears was answered by God! (Hebrews 5:7) "The hour" of suffering in the garden *did* pass. He was able to fulfill the purpose of his life and be "lifted up" publicly on the cross for all people to be drawn to him (John 12:32).

In the garden Jesus overcomes Satan. He overcomes fear and despair. He overcomes his cross.

Jesus gains the victory *before* he's crucified by watching and praying, by going to the cross *spiritually*. He's showing us how to watch and pray about our trials and temptations. Three times he prays, *"Abba,* Father... not what I will, but what you will." (Mark 14:36, 39, 41)

Jesus is falling into his Papa's arms of love.

Prayer

Identify a burden that's weighing you down and tell God how this feels for you...

Imagine Jesus with his arms open to you...

Lay your burden down and let your Savior hold you in Abba's love...

4th Station
Mary Comes to Jesus

*Thank you Jesus! By your cross
you gave us your life and showed us
how to love our mother.*

Meditation

"Simeon... said to Mary, [Jesus'] mother... 'A sword will pierce your own soul too.'" (Luke 2:34-35)

~

Probably Mary follows along close to her dear son as he carries his cross. We know that she stands close by his side as he is crucified (John 19:25-27). We know that, as Simeon prophesied, Jesus' cross becomes a sword that pierces her soul, cutting deeply into her mother's heart.

Mary has to accept that she can't take away Jesus' pain. It's so hard to see your loved one suffering and not be able to help!

But Mary does what she can for Jesus and it's beautiful: *she stays close to love her boy and she grows to worship him as her Lord and Savior, the Son of God!*

Mary's faith in Jesus Christ is a model for us all. She was the first to receive his incarnation when she offered her great prayer of submission: "May your word to me be fulfilled" (Luke 1:38).

From his earliest years on she treasured and pondered him in her heart (Luke 2:19). It was in response to her bold request that Jesus did his first public miracle of turning water into wine: she told the servants, "Do whatever [Jesus] tells you" (John 2:5).

Now as Jesus carries his cross through the streets of Jerusalem we can imagine that he might have made eye contact with Mary, as the ancient tradition indicates. What might he have said to his dear mother?

Perhaps something like, *Look mother,* "I am making everything new!" (Revelation 21:5)

Prayer

Thank God for your mother and how he blessed you through her...

Take heart from Mary's devotion and let yourself be drawn in closer to Jesus and his wounds...

Ask God to use the cross of Christ to cut out of your soul anything that distracts you from loving him and your neighbors...

5th Station
Simon "Helps" Jesus Carry His Cross

*Thank you Jesus! By your cross
you gave us your life and showed us
the power of companionship in suffering.*

Meditation

"A certain man from Cyrene, Simon, the father of Alexander and Rufus, was passing by on his way in from the country, and they forced him to carry the cross" (Mark 15:21).

~

Simon is picked out of the crowd, pulled away from his sons, and "forced" to carry Jesus' heavy cross. Now the crowds are jeering at him too! Now the soldiers are abusing him too!

No doubt Simon is bitterly angry!

But apparently he comes to accept his identification with Jesus and to consider it an honor to "help" him carry his cross.

It seems that watching Jesus suffer and die with perfect love for everyone, even his enemies, impels Simon and his sons to put their trust in him as their Lord and Savior and to learn from him how to love all people (Romans 16:13).

So really *it is Jesus who helps Simon!*

Usually when we suffer we feel alone and sorry for ourselves. But at this 5th Station of the Cross we're invited to realize that Christ has gone ahead of us and suffered first out of love for us (Romans 5:8).

Whatever injustice or pain you're experiencing, prayerfully consider how Jesus suffered something similar. Review his life in the Gospels and you'll find that you're not alone — Jesus went through that kind of trial out of love for you. *He's waiting to embrace you and empower you to overcome your difficulty!*

Paul called this "the participation in [Christ's] sufferings" and indicated it is the way into the "surpassing worth" of knowing Jesus more intimately. (Philippians 3:8-10)

Prayer

Consider something you feel forced to do or something that is unfair or painful to endure…

Recall how Jesus experienced something similar with his cross or earlier in his life and give thanks to him…

Pray to draw sweet nurture and divine strength from the companionship of Christ in your suffering…

6th Station
Veronica Wipes Jesus' Face

*Thank you Jesus! By your cross
you gave us your life and showed us
how to give and receive kindness.*

Meditation

"Whatever you did for one of the least of these brothers or sisters of mine, you did for me" (Matthew 25:40).

~

There's an ancient Christian legend that a woman named Veronica comes to Jesus as he carries his cross and she gives him a cloth to wipe his face of blood and sweat. When he gives the cloth back to her it has a blood-stained imprint of his face. This cloth is called "The Shroud of Turin."

This story is not in the Bible, but it's a lovely and inspiring legend that teaches a deep truth. Veronica means "true image." Her simple act of kindness reveals Christ to us. *We see his loving face in her service.*

Each of us are called to be "Christ's ambassadors" to other people in order to help them experience God's forgiveness and friendliness. The ministry of the Cross — Divine mercy, compassionate listening, reconciliation, and encouraging words — often come through people. (2 Corinthians 5:20-21)

This goes both ways. We need to give and receive this mediation of Christ's love. If we're not receiving grace through the body of Christ then we'll burn out in our ministry to others. If we're not giving grace to other people then it calls into question how much grace we've actually received.

Prayer

Consider if you've been so busy or stressed that you've neglected to stop and be kind to others...

Ask the Father to help you connect with the kindness of Christ and share this with others...

Pray that the lovely face of Christ would be revealed to you and those you care for...

7th Station
Jesus Falls Again

Thank you Jesus! By your cross you gave us your life and showed us the path of peace.

Meditation

"I am laid low in the dust." (Psalm 119:25).

"Surely he took up our [infirmities]... he was pierced for our transgressions... the punishment that brought us peace was on him, and by his wounds we are healed... He was led like a lamb to the slaughter." (Isaiah 53:4-5, 7)

~

According to the ancient tradition Jesus falls under the weight of his cross more than once. This can be seen as a symbol of how Jesus fulfills Isaiah's prophecy by bearing our sin and sickness.

The weight of our spiritual and physical dysfunctions is too much for us — we collapse and can't rise up in our own strength.

But Christ Jesus is the perfect "Lamb of God who takes away the sin of the world" (John 1:29). He took the punishment that we deserved so that we could be healed of our sins and the sins of others against us, freeing us from shame and isolation.

Jesus "fell" into our iniquity and infirmity, but it wasn't like somebody tripped him! He chose to take the fall for us. It was his great passion to take our sin upon himself and bear the consequences, even though he never sinned.

And he rose up from the dust by taking hold of the Father's hand that reached down to him.

Prayer

What burden of sin or sickness has laid you low in the dust?...

Ask God to minister the cross of Christ to you and deliver you (and anyone he brings to mind) from this heavy weight...

Pray to live in the peace of Christ — even if in your body or circumstances you're still hurting...

8th Station

Jesus Comforts the Weeping Women

*Thank you Jesus! By your cross
you gave us your life and showed us
how to grieve and find lasting comfort.*

Meditation

"A large number of people followed [Jesus], including women who mourned and wailed for him. Jesus turned and said to them, 'Daughters of Jerusalem, do not weep for me; weep for yourselves and for your children.'" (Luke 23:27-28)

~

When we see the terrible suffering of Jesus in his passion probably we feel sad for him like these mothers did. The brutality is so gruesome and his pain is so overwhelming! We may start to feel depressed.

But there is another, deeper reality and Jesus re-directs our vision to it.

In effect, he says to the weeping women and to us: "Look. I'm doing fine. My Father is sustaining me. I'm choosing to go to the cross for you. So don't cry for me — cry *to* me. Cry for yourselves and the people you know to be delivered of sin and to receive God's mercy."

Is Jesus denying his pain? Of course not! He feels horrific pain. He cries out repeatedly.

The point is that our Master and Messiah has prepared himself to endure this pain out of love for us. He's concerned to help us with our pain and especially with our sin.

Jesus is teaching these mothers and us how to grieve. Healthy grief is not about feeling bad or depressed — it's about feeling *sad* and *seeking empathy* because of our sins and faults (2 Corinthians 7:10-11). We also need to grieve and seek comfort over ways we've been sinned against, or when a loved one dies, or when we suffer any kind of loss (e.g., Psalms 126 and 137).

To feel downcast for Jesus because of the gruesome suffering of his cross is to miss his heart. He wants us to realize how broken and needy we are and to cry out to him to receive his forgiveness and lovingkindness.

Jesus wants us to open our hearts to receive God's healing mercy and share it with others.

Prayer

Reflect on an experience in which you (or a loved one) feel distressed or discouraged...

Ask God to help you not be depressed about this but instead to feel sad and to seek Christ's care...

Pray that these hurts would become "sacred wounds" that God sanctifies to use in ministry to others who hurt in a similar way...

9th Station

Jesus Falls a Third Time

*Thank you Jesus! By your cross
you gave us your life and showed us
how to rise again when we fall down.*

Meditation

"Though the righteous fall seven times, they rise again..." (Proverbs 24:16).

"Christ Jesus... being in very nature God, did not consider equality with God something to be used to his own advantage; rather, he made himself nothing, by taking the very nature of a servant, being made in human likeness. And being found in appearance as a man, he humbled himself by becoming obedient to death — even death on a cross!" (Philippians 2:5-8)

~

According to the ancient tradition of The Stations, as Jesus staggers to carry his cross to Calvary he falls again and again and *again*. The point of this is not historical accuracy but spiritual meditation.

We recall how we've fallen down in life. We consider Jesus' human limitations and the weight of his cross.

Scourged nearly to death. Carrying his cross. *Becoming our sin offering.* Jesus is stretched beyond his manly abilities so he depends entirely on God his Father.

That Jesus falls three times is significant. In holy love our Lord "took the fall" for us into our sin, our death, and our hell. He overcame the three awful enemies that threaten to destroy us! (Revelation 1:18)

We need to pray about each of these dangers and put our trust in Christ who delivers us.

Jesus transforms our badness into his divine goodness!

He heals our alienation to reconcile us into his oneness with God!

He redirects our eternal destiny from the hell we deserve to the heaven that only he deserves!

Prayer

Confess your sinfulness to the Lord and seek his forgiveness...

Give thanks to God for delivering you from death into life...

Pray for someone who needs to trust in Christ for salvation from sin...

42 Unforsaken!

10th Station
The Soldiers Strip and Abuse Jesus

*Thank you Jesus! By your cross
you gave us your life and showed us
how to overcome abuse with dignity.*

Meditation

"The governor's soldiers took Jesus into the Praetorium and gathered the whole company of soldiers around him. They stripped him... and mocked him... and struck him on the head again and again... Then they led him away to crucify him." (Matthew 27:27-31)

"Jesus said, 'Father, forgive them'... And they divided up his clothes by casting lots. The people stood watching, and the rulers even sneered at him." (Luke 23:34-35)

~

If you've ever been called bad names, yelled at, hit, or violated sexually then the Tenth Station of the Cross is especially for you. Here Christ suffers as you have, but even worse, and his divine empathy and mercy bleed out to minister personal healing to you.

Furthermore, maybe you realize that you've mistreated others and need Christ's mercy for your sins.

By trusting in Christ at the cross you can experience spiritual and emotional healing, forgiveness and freedom. Also you can be empowered to share his mercy and love with others — even your enemies.

Luke shows us how Jesus forgives and loves the soldiers who spit on him, slap him, and strike him repeatedly with their fists. Is he just being a doormat? Helpless and afraid? Ashamed to be abused?

No! When our Lord turns the other cheek and blesses those that curse him (as he taught us to do in Luke 6:27-30) — he's strong and confident.

In John's account of the Passion we repeatedly see that Jesus is bold to speak the truth in love to his abusers (John 18 and 19). For instance, when the high priest's official slaps Jesus in the face our Lord turns his cheek by saying, "If I said something wrong, testify as to what is wrong. But if I spoke the truth, why did you strike me?" (John 18:22-23)

Prayer

Reflect on your memories and emotions in response to the abuse that Jesus endured...

Pray for God to heal you of hurt, shame, anger, and fear...

Pray that you'd be so released and renewed that you'd have increasing capacity to forgive and love others as God has done for you in Jesus Christ...

11th Station

Jesus is Crucified With Two Thieves

*Thank you Jesus! By your cross
you gave us your life and showed us
how to access and share Paradise!*

Meditation

"They crucified [Jesus], along with the criminals — one on his right, the other on his left... One of the criminals who hung there hurled insults at him: 'Aren't you the Messiah? Save yourself and us!'

"But the other criminal rebuked him. 'Don't you fear God?... Then he said, 'Jesus, remember me when you come into your kingdom.'

"Jesus answered him, "Today you will be with me in paradise." (Luke 23:33, 39-43)

~

It's never too late for God's good purposes to be fulfilled in your life or that of a loved one! It's never too late to learn to experience *eternal living* with Christ! "Now is the day of salvation" (2 Corinthians 6:2).

Look at Jesus on his cross between the two thieves on their crosses. All three are being tortured to death. Jesus' suffering is infinitely worse because he is also bearing our sin — yet he is the one who is extending compassion and forgiveness to everyone around him!

As Jesus suffers he is drawing nurture and power from his Father's storehouse in the heavenly realms. That's what he always does. It's the kind of person he is.

In contrast, the two thieves have no connection to God in the heavens and so they're writhing in bitterness and spewing out curses (Matthew 27:44).

However, later one of the thieves is so drawn in by observing the goodness and grace of Christ that he is convicted of his sin and cries out for God's mercy just before he dies (Luke 23:42).

Immediately that thief's suffering is diminished and redeemed by the divine life, love, glory, and power that flow into him. Soon he'll enter into eternal paradise!

Prayer

What trial is causing you (or a loved one) distress? Offer this to the Lord...

Pray with the repentant thief: "Jesus, remember _(name)_ when you enter your kingdom."

Give thanks to God for Paradise! And for heavenly graces flowing to you *now!*

Unforsaken! 49

12th Station
Mary and John Watch Jesus Die

*Thank you Jesus! By your cross
you gave us your life and showed us
how to trust God when we feel forsaken.*

Meditation

"At noon, darkness came over the whole land until three in the afternoon. [Then] Jesus cried out in a loud voice... 'My God, my God, why have you forsaken me?'" (Mark 15:33-34; Psalm 22:1)

"When Jesus saw his mother there, and the disciple whom he loved standing nearby, he said to her, '[Dear] woman, here is your son,' and to the disciple, 'Here is your mother.'" (John 19:26-27)

"One of the soldiers pierced Jesus' side with a spear, bringing a sudden flow of blood and water. The man who saw it... testifies so that you also may believe." (John 19:34-35)

~

Mark in his Gospel gives us only one of the seven last words of Jesus on the cross: his cry of abandonment.

It seems that God has forsaken Jesus on the cross (see also Isaiah 53:5-6, 10). So his followers feel forsaken too.

What's happening? The traditional view is that when Jesus took on our sin at the cross in order to reconcile us to God, who is holy and just, he experienced separation from God *for a time* as the consequence of our sin. Because of Jesus we are accepted by God.

Others say that Jesus only *felt* forsaken by God. Along these lines, when Jesus quoted the cry of abandonment in Psalm 22:1 he may have been invoking the whole psalm. This Messianic prophecy goes on to say, "For [the LORD] has not despised or scorned the suffering of the afflicted one; he has not hidden his face from him but has listened to his cry for help." (v 24)

Luke's view of the cross emphasizes this bond between Father and Son. He doesn't record a cry of abandonment, but shows Jesus totally trusting in his Father's loving care as he suffers (23:45-46; see also Acts 2:25-33).

We'll never fully understand the mysteries of how Jesus earned our salvation from sin! But we can be sure that our Lord wants us to join him in trusting the God who will never leave us nor forsake us (Deuteronomy 31:6; Hebrews 13:5).

In John's gospel, as Jesus hung on the cross, and just before his victorious cry of "It is finished!" (19:30), he asks Mary and John to love one another as mother and son. He's empathizing with how they feel abandoned by God and offering comfort.

Very soon he'll no longer be physically present with them they'll need to help one another learn to rely on his *spiritual* presence.

Like Mary and John, we need to go to the cross and find a soul friend. We can help one another to trust that joined together in Christ we are truly *Unforsaken!*

Prayer

What friend helps you to stay close to Christ at the cross?

Thank God for this friend and the things you especially appreciate about him or her…

Pray that you'd help each other always to depend on the Spirit of Jesus and to be devoted to him…

13th Station

Jesus' Body is Taken Off the Cross

*Thank you Jesus! By your cross
you gave us your life and showed us
how to abandon our life to the Father.*

Meditation

"[Mary] wrapped him in cloths..." (Luke 2:7)

"Jesus called out with a loud voice, 'Father, into your hands I commit my spirit.' When he had said this, he breathed his last.

"The centurion, seeing what had happened, praised God...

"The women who had followed him from Galilee stood at a distance watching...

"Going to Pilate, [Joseph of Arimathea] asked for Jesus' body. Then he took it down and wrapped it in linen cloth... " (Luke 23:46-47, 49, 52-53)

~

Joseph of Arimathea had been a secret follower of Jesus because he was a member of the Sanhedrin. But now he discards his reputation and goes *boldly* to Pilate to ask for his Lord's body. Then he carefully takes it down from the cross.

Nicodemus, also a member of the Sanhedrin coming out publicly as a disciple of Christ, brings spices for the body and together they embalm him (John 19:38-42). The women who cared for Jesus' needs when he was alive also care for his body now (Matthew 27:55-56).

According to tradition, Mary the mother of Jesus was one of these women. Michelangelo's famous Pietà statue depicts her tenderly holding the dead body of her son. No longer is he on the cross in excruciating pain — now he looks at peace, laying still in his mother's arms. This may not be historical, but any mother who goes through the trauma of burying a child recalls holding that child as an infant.

The Pietà is a precious picture that portrays Jesus' complete relinquishment to God as his Abba.

Jesus lived every moment with that *total trust* in his Father. He never tried to control people or situations; he didn't try to force things to happen but kept abandoning outcomes to God; he always acted and spoke in concert with his Father's will. (John 5:19, 6:38, 12:50)

Trying to get people to do things or to control outcomes of situations causes us a lot of stress! Also it's offensive to people. But

Jesus' way of relinquishment to God brings great peace to us and the people around us.

Our Teacher's final cross prayer of submission to God came from his Prayer Book. He prayed Psalm 31:5: Father, "into your hands I commit my spirit." (Luke 23:46)

This is a powerful prayer and here's a practical way to pray it:

Prayer

Identify a situation in which you want to control the outcome...

Tell God how you feel about this...

Then join with Jesus to submit this situation to God by gently repeating his prayer: "Father, into your hands I commit _(name of person, event, or thing)_ ."

14th Station

Joseph Puts Jesus' Body Into His Tomb

Thank you Jesus! By your cross you gave us your life and showed us how to die.

Meditation

"Joseph... placed [Jesus' body] in a tomb cut out of rock. Then he rolled a stone against the entrance of the tomb. Mary Magdalene and Mary the mother of Joseph saw where he was laid." (Mark 15:46-47)

~

Joseph doesn't want Jesus' body discarded in a mass grave or burned in the Roman way. He wants to give his Lord a proper burial in the Hebrew way. In the garden near the crucifixion site there is a new tomb in a rock cave and so he uses this (John 19:41). Probably it is Joseph's tomb.

Imagine Joseph carrying Jesus' dead body into the darkness of his own grave! He must feel erie anticipations of his own death mingled in with his grief over his Lord's death.

The ancient Christians used Bible texts like the account of Jesus' burial to help them meditate on their death. It may seem strange to us to pray this way, but it's not unlike attending a funeral or reading the obituaries and being prayerful as you do these things.

The Psalmist invites us to contemplate our death to help us live for God in the "here and now." He prays, "O LORD, show me the end of my life and that my days are numbered. Help me to know how fleeting my life is… Truly each person is but a breath. *Selah.*" (Psalm 39:4, 11; paraphrased)

In another Psalm we consider our earthly life as puff of smoke that blows away in the wind. This is to inspire us to live today in the wonderful and eternal spiritual reality where the Lord is enthroned. (Psalm 102:3, 12)

Prayer

Ask God to help you prepare for your death and wisely number the days on earth that he gives you (Psalm 90:12)…

Imagine your body being put into a dark tomb like Jesus' was…

See the white sheet laid over your body and receive it as a symbol of the Spirit of Christ covering you and holding you…

60 *Unforsaken!*

Note: During Lent it's helpful to save the 15th Station until Easter Sunday and following.

15th Station
Jesus Rises From the Dead!

*Thank you Jesus! By your cross
you gave us your life and showed us
how to live with your resurrection power!*

Meditation

"When the Sabbath was over, Mary Magdalene, Mary the mother of James, and Salome bought spices so that they might go to anoint Jesus' body...

"They saw that the stone, which was very large, had been rolled away. As they entered the tomb, they saw a young man dressed in a white robe sitting on the right side, and they were alarmed.

"'Don't be alarmed,' he said. 'You are looking for Jesus the Nazarene, who was crucified. He has risen! He is not here. See the place where they laid him. But go, tell his disciples and Peter, 'He is going ahead of you into Galilee. There you will see him, just as he told you." (Mark 16:1, 4-7)

"Christ lives in me!" (Galatians 2:20)

~

The original ending of Mark leaves us in suspense. The women run from the tomb "trembling and bewildered" (verse 8).

The implicit question that Mark leaves us with is: *Wow will you respond to the empty tomb? How will you live each day?*

We may believe the historical fact of Jesus' resurrection and yet not know how to participate in the divine life that the risen Christ is now living in our daily life.

It's easy for us to make the mistake of separating our "spiritual life" (like our church activities, devotions, or ministry) from the rest of our lives (like our business, home, friendships, or entertainment).

But our school of discipleship to Jesus is not religious activities — it's *all* of our daily life activities. Our opportunity is to learn to live *one whole life* in the presence of and under the leadership of the Spirit of the risen Christ.

We need to hear and obey the word of the angel to Mary Magdalene and the other women: "Jesus has risen! He is going ahead of you."

That's when the great God-adventure of life begins! It's as we draw life from abiding in the Spirit of Jesus and his word, waiting and watching for his movement, and keeping in step with him (John 15:7; Galatians 5:25).

Prayer

Consider a personal challenge in your life in which you need to appreciate that the risen Christ is present to bless you and guide you…

Appreciate and abide in the loving presence of the risen Christ who lives in you…

Ask God to guide your decisions and actions in this situation and wait on his leading. Imagine this by praying the angel's words, "The Spirit of Christ goes ahead of me into (name the situation) ."

~

Share the traditional Easter greeting with a friend. Exclaim, "Christ is risen!"

Await your friend's reply, "He is risen indeed!"

Appendix 1

Using *Unforsaken* in Lent (a Schedule)

You can use *Unforsaken* during Lent for personal devotions, small groups, or a sermon series. Starting with the Sunday before Ash Wednesday and concluding with Easter there are eight Sundays in Lent.

Week	Station	Key Scriptures
1 Ash Wed	1 2	Mark 15:1-15; Rom 8:1 John 19:17; Heb 12:1-3; Luke 9:23-27
2	3 4	Ps 38:5-12; Mark 14:32-42; John 12:27-33 Luke 1:38, 2:19, 2:34-35
3	5 6	Mark 15:21-22; Rom 5:8 Matt 25:31-46; 2 Cor 5:20-21

Week	Station	Key Scriptures
4	7 8	Ps 119:25; Isa 53; John 1:29 Luke 23:31-46; 2 Cor 7:10-11
5	9 10	Prov 24:16; Phil 2:5-11 Matt 27:27-31; Luke 23:34-35; John 18:22-23
6	11 12	Luke 23:32-43; 2 Cor 6:2 Ps 22:1, 24; Mark 15:33-34; John 19:25-37
7 Palm Sun Holy Week	13 14	Luke 2:7, 23:44-56 Ps 39:4, 11; Mark 15:42-47
8 Easter	15	Mark 16:1-8; Gal 2:20

Appendix 2

Scriptural Way Of the Cross

Of the original fifteen Stations of the Cross that are used in *Unforsaken!* (including the resurrection) there are ten that come directly from the Bible. But what about the other five?

Three Stations (3, 7, and 9) focus on Jesus falling under the weight of cross which is inferred from Mark 15:21 where Simon of Cyrene comes to help Jesus carry his cross. Probably Jesus didn't fall three times, but this is repeated in The Stations to further our appreciation for the ways that Jesus "took the fall" for us and to consider the ways that we fall down in life and need to be lifted back up.

Station 4 has Jesus meeting his mother Mary during his Cross walk. This is not in the Bible, but it may have happened and it reminds us of what the Scriptures do say about their relationship. It's a very heart-warming story that gives us an emotional break from the suffering of the cross.

Station 6, which features Veronica giving Jesus a cloth to wipe his face of blood and sweat, is a legend. This is another respite during the "Way of Suffering." It's a lovely myth that teaches the Biblical value of kindness and the importance of gaining a true image of Christ Jesus.

Speaking of rest points on the Way of Suffering, in Station 12 (Mary and John Watch Jesus Die) we focus on the Biblical account of Jesus connecting his beloved mother and disciple to care for each other after he dies.

Station 13 is based on the Biblical account of Joseph of Arimathea taking Jesus' body down from the cross. In my devotional I have added the story of Mary cradling the body of her dead son (as depicted in Michaelangelo's Pietà). We don't know if this happened, but it's an endearing story that invites a profitable meditation on holding Christ in our hearts.

To align The Stations of the Cross more closely with the Bible a number of adaptations have been developed. In 1991 Pope John Paul II sanctioned "The Scriptural Way of the Cross" as an official Roman Catholic version:

1. Jesus in the Garden of Gethsemane
2. Jesus is betrayed by Judas and arrested
3. Jesus is condemned by the Sanhedrin
4. Jesus is denied by Peter
5. Jesus is judged by Pilate
6. Jesus is scourged and crowned with thorns
7. Jesus takes up his cross
8. Jesus is helped by Simon to carry his cross
9. Jesus meets the women of Jerusalem
10. Jesus is crucified
11. Jesus promises his kingdom to the thief
12. Jesus entrusts Mary and John to each other
13. Jesus dies on the cross
14. Jesus is laid in the tomb

Made in the USA
San Bernardino, CA
22 February 2017